HEALING IS YOUR PORTION JOURNAL

Moving from Your to My, A Personal Journey Within

By Tammy Toney-Butler

Table of Contents

Dedication

First, God deserves all the glory and praise in my life. I am nothing without His grace and mercy. I was dead, a shell of a person, until He saw fit to set me free, transform my mind and body, and make me a new creature in Christ. This book is a Holy Spirit-inspired download, written as I embraced my new identity in Christ Jesus and fully stepped into the call God placed on my life as a Healing Evangelist. It is His masterpiece, and as you read it, please see Him as the author and not me.

Next, I want to thank David, my husband, who stayed with me and showed me what real love was about. A love that embraced the messy believed in my causes and steadied my troubled soul. A love that refused to quit on me when I was caught in an emotional flashback and full of the residue of trauma, dressed in shame-soaked, icky garments full of holes. David offered no judgment, just praise and unconditional love, providing hope that a girl like me, broken, could be worthy of love and sustain it. David empowered me to become the real me and supported me financially until I broke free of the past, and into all God purposed me to become as a warrior for His Kingdom.

Additionally, David's parents are Russ and Seda. Parents who loved me despite my messiness and showed me what it means to be part of a family. Always in my corner, full of unconditional praise and encouragement. Seda, always dressing me for every occasion, and most of all for giving life to their son, David.

To my mother, Dianne, I give thanks. A few weeks before she died, after we prayed, she permitted me to discuss our life, unfiltered, if it would save another family from being destroyed by generational trauma—a mother who made choices based on survival from a trauma-soaked lens—a mother whom I loved dearly despite her failure to mother me as I deserved. A mother who I know now is in heaven, with my baby sister Anita, and would be so proud of the woman I have become in Christ Jesus. My mother never stopped praising Jesus.

Now, to my father, Marcel, who never really survived Vietnam, and struggled with addiction, coping through alcoholism, and serving through his hidden pain, and helping many as a police officer. A father who lost his battle with complex PTSD suffered in silence until he died with a self-inflicted gunshot wound (suicide) when I was age fifteen, and we buried him on Father's Day. Please reach out for help to all those suffering in silence. The world is a much better place with you in it. A daughter always longs for her father, even if he cannot be one. I loved my dad despite his not being able to parent me as I deserved. I know he would have been proud of me. I was proud of him despite his messiness.

Next, to my baby sister, Anita, who went home to be with the Lord in 2025. She suffered much but loved much. She was my encourager, and despite our being apart for most of her life, separated by lost promises and broken environments, my love for her never ceased, as did my love for my other siblings. Trauma destroyed my family, and as I journey to keep it from destroying yours, I carry Anita with me. She was strong, despite her body failing her in the aftermath of trauma and coping through various addictions. She was homeless at times, trafficked as a child and adult, had an arrest record, and never spoke of all she endured. As they amputated lower limb by lower limb due to vascular issues, she was in and out of the hospital, and through it all, she remained devoted to and praising the Lord Jesus. I love you, Anita. I will see you again.

Furthermore, to all my brothers and sisters in Christ, I would be nothing without your prayers and love. United, we are stronger. We must be the Light!

Now, to every educator (schoolteacher, principal) who poured into me as a child and influenced my path. You know who you are, and I owe you so much that words could never convey!

Finally, to all the "thrivers" and "overcomers" who have made it and are sowing those seeds of hope. Keep it up, for the harvest is great, and the laborers are few. Keep shining your Light and stay strong as we navigate the darkness of this world. Find your voice and use it! In all things give thanks and pray without ceasing.

Healing is Your Portion: A Disciple's Guide to Healing

Healing Is Your Portion: A Disciple's Guide to Healing, examines the biblical foundations and practical applications of divine healing within a Christian context. It examines essential topics such as the role of scripture in providing irrefutable evidence for divine healing, the impact of unforgiveness on wholeness, the faith required for the restoration of health, and spiritual practices, including the laying on of hands and anointing with oil. Additionally, it highlights the significance of a healer's anointing, the operation of spiritual gifts, and the redemptive work of the Cross, culminating in prayers and concluding insights. The material aims to provide readers with a comprehensive understanding of divine healing through the lens of faith, providing a reference manual for miracles highlighted in the Bible, both the Old and New Testaments, accounts, as well as practical steps to incorporate these healing principles into their everyday lives, ministries, and discipleship programs.

Introduction to Journal

This book is designed to accompany Healing Is Your Portion: A Disciple's Guide to Divine Healing, enhancing learning, comprehension, and spiritual digestion of the material, guiding the reader from "Your Portion" to "My Portion." Creating a personal encounter with the Lord Jesus Christ, one page, one miracle of healing, at a time. A personal journey to wholeness, through the lens of faith, moving you from a reader to a doer, from a disciple to an apostle, from a soldier to a general, all through the power of the Lord Jesus Christ's Spirit that dwells within each of us.

We recognize this process can bring unease and be "triggering" for some. Please step out, take a break, have a drink or a snack, and proceed at your own pace. Holding a cold bottle of water in your hand can help ground you if you are at home alone while reading this content.

We have provided a link to hotline support at the back of this book if needed. Everyone responds differently to the content provided, and this course may not be a good fit for you. We respect that decision. Please refrain from participating if you are feeling distressed in any way. We are here to help, assist you on your healing journey, and are in no way mandating you read this book or complete its content.

We recognize everyone's journey is unique and highly personal, and that they transition through the stages of healing differently, as with the stages of grief. Cut yourself some slack. You are doing great. Walk at a snail's pace if that is what is needed.

We applaud your courage in purchasing Healing Is Your Portion and this workbook, and in attending our conferences, meetings, or services. We believe in you and are here to help if you need assistance.

Please let us know how we can pray for you and agree with you for your healing. You are not alone. You are seen and heard, have a voice, and are empowered to use it as you become a bold witness for Christ and attest to the healing that comes from knowing Him, believing in Him, and being guided by Him.

Record your journey as you go through this book in a journal. Answer the questions and participate in your healing. When you write things down, a release happens in your spirit, and you become lighter. You are surrendering those things to the Lord Jesus to take care of, releasing them, and bringing them out of the darkness and into the Light of His Truth. Thus, breaking a stronghold off your mind, loosening yourself from satan's grip on your life.

Chapter 1: Is Healing for Everyone?

Let's start by asking yourself if you can accept this declaration into your heart? Do you sense hesitancy within you about whether you can be personally set free from the past? When Tammy says, "healing is for everyone," does she mean you? Ask the Holy Spirit to reveal to you any hindrances to your own personal healing and transformation? Write them down in this section, and we will discuss them in greater detail in our table discussions if you are attending one of our healing meetings, conferences, or services. If you are reading this alone, at home, and not part of a healing group, consider attending one of our conferences or meetings and join a tribe of broken vessels mended by the Great Physician, Lord Jesus Christ, who are blazing a trail of freedom across the world. Journal at home the answers to these questions.

1. Is healing for me? If yes, why? If, no, why? When you read that statement, do any emotions well up inside of you, good or bad?

2. What do you believe is stopping you or hindering your healing journey? Letting go of past hurts? People? Places?

One of the most challenging things we can get asked to do is to let go of the unforgiveness we hold towards someone who has wronged us. As a survivor of child sex trafficking, I understand this all too well. Forgiving my mother was a long process, only done by the strength found in Jesus. When I finally realized she had her own unresolved childhood trauma and parented me in survival mode based on trauma responses, I was able to show her grace. She endured many hardships as a child; most she never spoke of, not even when she was close to death. By realizing that Lord Jesus showed me mercy and God forgave my sins, I knew I had to extend her the same grace.[1]

Do you need to forgive someone? Do you need to let go of past hurts and unforgiveness so you can be whole? Remember, a blockage or hinderance to healing is unforgiveness. The time is now to forgive them, and you have my permission to forgive yourself!

Journal what you are feeling? Are you able to let go? If you need help, remember the Holy Spirit is our advocate, helper, comforter, and physician. Call on Him to help. Say, Holy Spirit, help me to forgive them and help me to forgive myself.

---

[1] Healing Is Your Portion: A Disciple's Guide to Divine Healing, Page. 22. 2026 version, Tammy Toney-Butler.

Declarations

Healing is My Portion, say it aloud three times. Declare this Truth over yourself as must as you need to believe it! Meditate on these scriptures.

1 John 5:14-15
Complete Jewish Bible
14 This is the confidence we have in his presence: if we ask anything that accords with his will, he hears us. 15 And if we know that he hears us — whatever we ask — then we know that we have what we have asked from him.

Revelation 21:4
New International Version
4 'He will wipe every tear from their eyes. There will be no more death' or mourning or crying or pain, for the old order of things has passed away."

Jeremiah 17:14
King James Version (KJV)
14 Heal me, O Lord, and I shall be healed; save me, and I shall be saved: for thou art my praise.

Mark 5:34
The Message Bible (MSG)

34 Jesus said to her, "Daughter, you took a risk of faith, and now you're healed and whole. Live well, live blessed! Be healed of your plague."

Isaiah 53:5
New King James Version

5 But He was wounded for our transgressions,
He was bruised for our iniquities;
The chastisement for our peace was upon Him,
And by His stripes we are healed.

Matthew 15:21-28
Amplified Bible

28 Then Jesus answered her, "Woman, your faith [your personal trust and confidence in My power] is great; it will be done for you as you wish." And her daughter was healed from that moment.

Chapter 2: What Role Does Faith Play in Your Healing Journey?

Let's start by asking yourself if you have the same kind of faith the woman with the issue of blood had when she pushed herself through the crowd and touched the hem of His garment so she could be made whole? Do you believe that it is God's will for you be healed? Do you think you deserve a better life? Do you have the faith as a mustard seed to speak to the mountain in your life and cast it into the sea? What distractions are hindering your growth as a Christian, your faith walk, that need to be dealt with so you can receive healing by faith? What negative words spoken over you in the past, or you have talked over yourself, need to be uprooted so you can rise as the warrior God has called you to be and step into the fullness of life He has for you, which includes divine healing and restoration? Journal at home the answers to these questions.

1. Answer one of the questions above that pierces your heart, speaks to your soul, and that you want to bring out into the open so the darkness can leave you now?

2. Confess any hidden bitterness, unforgiveness, hatred, anger, or resentment that has entered your heart and list them in this section. List any offenses you hold towards others that you need to let go of. For example, I need to let go of unforgiveness for one of my parents, a co-worker, or a past intimate partner who hurt me.

Declarations

Healing is My Portion, say it aloud three times. Declare this Truth over yourself as must as you need to believe it! Rebuke cancer. Rebuke depression. Rebuke anxiety. Rebuke pain. Rebuke fatigue. Meditate on these scriptures.

James 5:14-15
Amplified Bible

14 Is anyone among you sick? He must call for the elders (spiritual leaders) of the church and they are to pray over him, anointing him with oil in the name of the Lord; 15 and the prayer of faith will restore the one who is sick, and the Lord will raise him up; and if he has committed sins, he will be forgiven.

Matthew 17:20
King James Version

20 And Jesus said unto them, Because of your unbelief: for verily I say unto you, If ye have faith as a grain of mustard seed, ye shall say unto this mountain, Remove hence to yonder place; and it shall remove; and nothing shall be impossible unto you.

Mark 5:34
Complete Jewish Bible (CJB)

34 "Daughter," he said to her, "your trust has healed you. Go in peace, and be healed of your disease."

Jeremiah 30:17
Amplified Bible
17

For I will restore health to you
And I will heal your wounds,' says the Lord,
Because they have called you an outcast, saying:
"This is Zion; no one seeks her and no one cares for her."

Psalm 147:3
Amplified Bible
3 He heals the brokenhearted
And binds up their wounds [healing their pain and comforting their
sorrow].

Deuteronomy 7:15
Amplified Bible
15 The Lord will take away from you all sickness; and He will not subject
you to any of the harmful diseases of Egypt which you have known, but He
will impose them on all [those] who hate you.

Jeremiah 29:11
New Living Translation
For I know the plans I have for you," says the LORD. "They are plans
for good and not for disaster, to give you a future and a hope.

Chapter 3: What Miracle of Healing in the Bible Resonated with You in a Personal Way?

We see in chapter three many miracles listed regarding healing and the restoration of life, either by literally raising them from the dead or spiritually by casting out tormenting demons or unclean spirits. What areas in your life do you need to surrender to the cleansing blood of Jesus, so you are free from tormenting thoughts or patterns of behavior, self-condemnation, imposter syndrome, self-sabotage, feelings of rejection, or addictions you are using to cope with the pains of yesterday? Journal at home the answers to these questions.

1. Answer the questions above here to the best of your ability. Some of us do not have memories from childhood, but sense something happened when we were younger. Whatever it is, whatever God lays on your heart, journal. Write it down as a form of release from its hold on you!

2. Do you have any "triggers" with these questions? Do they carry you off to a bad place or a good place? Write anything you are feeling here so we can expose those feelings to the Truth found in God's Word, the blood of Jesus, and bring healing to those wounds.

Declarations

Healing is My Portion, say it aloud three times. Declare this Truth over yourself as must as you need to believe it! Rebuke cancer. Rebuke depression. Rebuke anxiety. Rebuke pain. Rebuke fatigue. Rebuke addiction. Command them to go now, in the Name of Jesus! Meditate on these scriptures.

Exodus 15:26
New International Version
26 He said, "If you listen carefully to the Lord your God and do what is right in his eyes, if you pay attention to his commands and keep all his decrees, I will not bring on you any of the diseases I brought on the Egyptians, for I am the Lord, who heals you."

Acts 19:11-12
New King James Version
11 Now God worked unusual miracles by the hands of Paul, 12 so that even handkerchiefs or aprons were brought from his body to the sick, and the diseases left them and the evil spirits went out of them.

Chapter 4: Points of Contact for Healing

In chapter four, we read about the laying on of hands, anointing with oil, and touching garments or other items, all as points of transmission for healing. Do you believe these books are transmission points of healing, and by touching them and reading them, you are receiving divine healing? Do you recognize these as prophetic tools God uses to bring restoration and transformation to your door? You only need to believe and receive. Journal at home the answers to these questions.

1. Do you agree with question one above? If yes, why, and if no, why?

2. Do you agree with question two above? If yes, why, and if no, why?

3. What are you believing God for?

4. Journal what "Laying hands on" brings to the surface within you? Do you fear touch? Why? Where is the root?

Declarations

Healing is My Portion, say it aloud three times. Declare this Truth over yourself as must as you need to believe it! Rebuke cancer. Rebuke depression. Rebuke anxiety. Rebuke pain. Rebuke fatigue. Rebuke addiction. Command them to go now, in the Name of Jesus! Meditate on these scriptures.

John 14:12-14
New International Version

12 Very truly I tell you, whoever believes in me will do the works I have been doing, and they will do even greater things than these, because I am going to the Father. 13 And I will do whatever you ask in my name, so that the Father may be glorified in the Son. 14 You may ask me for anything in my name, and I will do it.

1 Peter 2:24
Tree of Life Version (TLV)

24 He Himself bore our sins in His body on the tree, so that we, removed from sins, might live for righteousness. "By His wounds you were healed."

Matthew 8:16-17
New International Version (NIV)

16 When evening came, many who were demon-possessed were brought to him, and he drove out the spirits with a word and healed all the sick. 17 This was to fulfill what was spoken through the prophet Isaiah:
"He took up our infirmities
and bore our diseases.

Isaiah 53:4-5
New International Version
4 Surely he took up our pain
and bore our suffering,
yet we considered him punished by God,
stricken by him, and afflicted.
5 But he was pierced for our transgressions,
he was crushed for our iniquities;
the punishment that brought us peace was on him,
and by his wounds we are healed.

Please journal what these scriptures mean to you and any emotions they bring to the surface.

James 5:16
Amplified Bible, Classic Edition
16 Confess to one another therefore your faults (your slips, your false steps, your offenses, your sins) and pray [also] for one another, that you may be healed and restored [to a spiritual tone of mind and heart]. The earnest (heartfelt, continued) prayer of a righteous man makes tremendous power available [dynamic in its working].

Chapter 5: Spiritual Discipline and Command Authority

Let's start by asking yourself if you walk in spiritual discipline. Are you Holy Spirit-led, or are you led by the world or by negative spirits such as bitterness, anger, pride, ego, or a need for approval from others? Do you live a "fasted lifestyle" and seek Him daily? Do you walk in a covenant relationship with the ability to command outcomes, speak to storms in your life, and demand they align with God's Word and will for your life? Do you realize that the Kingdom of Heaven is within you and you are seated in heavenly places with Christ Jesus, a daughter or son of the King? Journal at home the answers to these questions.

1. Do you seek God daily? Do you have a relationship with Him? Do demons tremble when you enter a room? Do you have a command presence? How do you know? Write anything you are feeling below as you ponder these questions. Use the additional pages provided to write on if needed.

2. What do you need to let go of to be more like Jesus? Are you willing to be led by the Holy Spirit? If not, why, be honest? He already knows what you're not saying out loud, writing down, or holding onto inside. Let it go! Use the additional pages provided to write on and get it out of you!

Declarations

Healing is My Portion, say it aloud three times. Declare this Truth over yourself as must as you need to believe it! Rebuke cancer. Rebuke depression. Rebuke anxiety. Rebuke pain. Rebuke fatigue. Rebuke addiction. Command them to go now, in the Name of Jesus! Meditate on these scriptures.

Luke 23:34
King James Version
34 Then said Jesus, Father, forgive them; for they know not what they do. And they parted his raiment, and cast lots.

Matthew 6:14-15
New International Version
14 For if you forgive other people when they sin against you, your heavenly Father will also forgive you. 15 But if you do not forgive others their sins, your Father will not forgive your sins.

Acts 7: 59-60
King James Version
59 And as they were stoning Stephen, he called out, "Lord Jesus, receive my spirit." 60 And falling to his knees he cried out with a loud voice, "Lord, do not hold this sin against them." And when he had said this, he fell asleep.

Acts 19:6
King James Version
6 And when Paul had laid his hands upon them, the Holy Ghost came on them; and they spake with tongues, and prophesied.

Chapter 6: Praising and Giving Thanks; The Cross is Enough

Do you enter His courts with praise and thanksgiving daily? Do you praise and worship Him regardless of your circumstances? Do you walk in gratitude and joy, with praise on your tongue, as you celebrate His work on the Cross and what He has already done for you, recognizing that the Cross was enough? He has already given you all you need to prosper, live a healthy, abundant life, free of sickness and disease, spiritual and physical freedom, but do you believe it? Will you receive the healing? Journal at home the answers to these questions.

1. Is healing for me? If yes, why? If, no, why? When you read that statement, do any emotions well up inside of you, good or bad? Use the additional pages provided to write on if needed. Get it out in the open.

2. What do you believe is stopping you or hindering your healing journey? Letting go of past hurts? People? Places? Use the additional pages provided to write on if needed.

Ephesians 6
English Standard Version
Children and Parents

6 Children, obey your parents in the Lord, for this is right. 2 "Honor your father and mother" (this is the first commandment with a promise), 3 "that it may go well with you and that you may live long in the land." 4 Fathers, do not provoke your children to anger, but bring them up in the discipline and instruction of the Lord.

Isaiah 58:8
Amplified Bible

8 "Then your light will break out like the dawn,
And your healing (restoration, new life) will quickly spring forth;
Your righteousness will go before you [leading you to peace and prosperity],
The glory of the Lord will be your rear guard

Ephesians 4:26-27
King James Version

26 Be ye angry, and sin not: let not the sun go down upon your wrath:
27 Neither give place to the devil.

Please journal what these scriptures mean to you and any emotions they bring to the surface.

Mother Thersa once said, "There is a light in this world, a healing spirit more powerful than any darkness we may encounter. We sometimes lose sight of this force when there is suffering, too much pain. Then suddenly, the spirit will emerge through the lives of ordinary people who hear a call and answer in extraordinary ways."[2] We must never forget to give thanks for the Light of the World, King Jesus.[3] Jesus's death on the Cross gives us all the reason we need to be full of joy and have a heart of gratitude. Meditate on this scripture and Journal what it means to you and the person you are becoming.

John 3:16 (NIV)

16 For God so loved the world that he gave his one and only Son, that whoever believes in him shall not perish but have eternal life.

---

[2] https://www.azquotes.com/quote/437765
[3] John 8:12 (English Standard Version)

Personal Declaration

Now, declare over yourself, out loud for all to hear: Healing is My Portion. Repeat it out loud again: "Healing is My Portion." Repeat it one last time, out loud: Healing is My Portion. That is a prophetic declaration you just made over your life. God gives us the desires of our hearts, and it is His will for your life that you walk in total freedom; no longer in Egypt, and Egypt no longer in you! Now, is there any area in your physical body that needs to come into alignment with God's Word and the declaration you just made over yourself? What about in your spirit man? Remember, we are spirit beings with a body and a soul (mind, will, and emotions). Our human spirit is invaded by the Holy Spirit when we surrender to the Lord Jesus as our Savior, enter the Kingdom of God through salvation, and ask the Holy Spirit to dwell in us and make us more like Christ. Our human spirit then aligns with the Holy Spirit that rises within us as we put our flesh under and surrender to the Holy Spirit's leading and prompting in our lives. Be Spirit-Led, Surrender, Obey! Break free now! Say, " I am free." Repeat it aloud: "I am free." Declare it one more time: "I am free." Now, journal. Record the day and hour you gained freedom, and transitioned from doubting to believing, and from believing to receiving.

Now, declare over yourself, out loud for all to hear: Healing is My Portion. Repeat it out loud again: "Healing is My Portion." Repeat it one last time, out loud: Healing is My Portion. That is a prophetic declaration you just made over your life.

Scriptures About Healing

Matthew 10:1
Amplified Bible

10 Jesus summoned His twelve disciples and gave them authority and power over unclean spirits, to cast them out, and to heal every kind of disease and every kind of sickness.

Mark 11:22-26
Amplified Bible

22 Jesus replied, "Have faith in God [constantly]. 23 I assure you and most solemnly say to you, whoever says to this mountain, 'Be lifted up and thrown into the sea!' and does not doubt in his heart [in God's unlimited power], but believes that what he says is going to take place, it will be done for him [in accordance with God's will]. 24 For this reason I am telling you, whatever things you ask for in prayer [in accordance with God's will], believe [with confident trust] that you have received them, and they will be given to you. 25 Whenever you stand praying, if you have anything against anyone, forgive him [drop the issue, let it go], so that your Father who is in heaven will also forgive you your transgressions and wrongdoings [against Him and others]. 26 [But if you do not forgive, neither will your Father in heaven forgive your transgressions."

Ephesians 4: 31-32
New international Version
31 Get rid of all bitterness, rage and anger, brawling and slander, along with every form of malice. 32 Be kind and compassionate to one another, forgiving each other, just as in Christ God forgave you.

Matthew 4:23
Amplified Bible
23 And He went throughout all Galilee, teaching in their synagogues and preaching the good news (gospel) of the kingdom, and healing every kind of disease and every kind of sickness among the people [demonstrating and revealing that He was indeed the promised Messiah].

Malachi 4:2
Amplified Bible
2 But for you who fear My name [with awe-filled reverence] the sun of righteousness will rise with healing in its wings. And you will go forward and leap [joyfully] like calves [released] from the stall.

Jeremiah 33:6
Amplified Bible
6 Behold, [in the restored Jerusalem] I will bring to it health and healing, and I will heal them; and I will reveal to them an abundance of peace (prosperity, security, stability) and truth.

Psalm 147:3
Amplified Bible
3 He heals the brokenhearted
And binds up their wounds [healing their pain and comforting
their sorrow].

Psalm 107:20
New International Version[4]
20 He sent out his word and healed them;
he rescued them from the grave.

Isaiah 58:8
Amplified Bible
8 "Then your light will break out like the dawn,
And your healing (restoration, new life) will quickly spring forth;
Your righteousness will go before you [leading you to peace and
prosperity],
The glory of the Lord will be your rear guard.

Seek out a quiet place and get alone with the Lord Jesus. Ask
Him to reveal to you what these passages of scripture mean.
Ask the Holy Spirit for wisdom and understanding. Journal
what He reveals to you through the Word of God.

---

[4] New International Version (Holy Bible, 1973, 1978, 1984, 2011, Biblica, Inc, BibleGateway.com)

James 5:16
Amplified Bible, Classic Edition

16 Confess to one another therefore your faults (your slips, your false steps, your offenses, your sins) and pray [also] for one another, that you may be healed and restored [to a spiritual tone of mind and heart]. The earnest (heartfelt, continued) prayer of a righteous man makes tremendous power available [dynamic in its working].

1 John 5:14-15
Complete Jewish Bible[5]

14 This is the confidence we have in his presence: if we ask anything that accords with his will, he hears us. 15 And if we know that he hears us — whatever we ask — then we know that we have what we have asked from him.

Revelation 21:4
New International Version

4 'He will wipe every tear from their eyes. There will be no more death' or mourning or crying or pain, for the old order of things has passed away.'

Jeremiah 17:14
King James Version (KJV)[6]

14 Heal me, O Lord, and I shall be healed; save me, and I shall be saved:

---

[5] Complete Jewish Bible (1998, David H. Stern, BibleGateway.com)
[6] King James Version (Public Domain)

Prayers and Declarations of Healing

Father, heal me Father, heal me according to your word. I know by Jesus's work on the Cross that healing is my portion. According to Isaiah 53:5 and Jeremiah 17:14, I know with this prayer, I am healed. I believe it according to Your Word and thank you for the healing that has entered my body now. I praise Your holy name. In the mighty name of Jesus Christ, I pray and declare all things, by His blood shed on Calvary, I am healed!

Amen

Father, according to Psalm 30:2, Psalm 107:20, and Isaiah 40:31, I receive my healing and walk in divine strength. My strength is renewed like the eagles, and I have health in my body and nourishment in my bones, as it says in Proverbs 3:7-8. You are a good Father who will never leave nor forsake me, and I thank you that you are with me now and have heard my cries. I am walking in divine health now and know cancer is not my portion. I bind cancer and loose divine health in the name of Lord Jesus Christ.

Amen

Father, I thank You that You heard me and have healed me. I praise You for sending Your Son, Lord Jesus, to die on the Cross for me, a sinner. I give You all honor and Glory and praise Jesus for His yes, so I could be set free from sin, sickness, and eternal death. I agree with Your Word, that "By His Stripes, Ye were Healed." I see that it is past tense, and it is for me, recognizing that nothing else needs to be done for me to receive my healing. Jesus did the work over two thousand years ago on the Cross, and I believe, with this prayer and declaration, that I am healed. Healing is My Portion. It is finished. In Jesus mighty name.

Amen

A Daily Dose of Healing

Many of you have suffered or are currently struggling to overcome an ailment or two such as chronic pain, chronic fatigue, anxiety, depression, shame, guilt, fear, regret, self-loathing, and the list could go on and on. Today, let's arm ourselves with the Truth found in God's Word, and speak to those ailments and command them to Go! In the Name of Jesus.

Each day, declare these scriptures aloud and demand the enemy leave you alone. You have been healed by the Blood of Jesus. Resist the devil, and he shall flee. So, we are resisting him now by our sword, the Word of God. Go to war, warriors, against those ailments above.

Speak life over yourself. Build yourself up in the faith. Build others up in the faith. Remember, to praise and worship daily, despite your circumstances. Be grateful for the work Jesus has already done on the Cross for our healing over two thousand years ago.

Check out Tammy Toney-Butler's YouTube channel, Reflective Hour, and search for A Daily Dose of Healing Podcast and Video Series. Go to www.reflectivehour.com

Rebuke Pain and Discomfort

Jeremiah 29:11
King James Version

11 For I know the thoughts that I think toward you, saith the LORD, thoughts of peace, and not of evil, to give you an expected end.

Mark 9:23-24
King James Version

23 Jesus said unto him, If thou canst believe, all things are possible to him that believeth.

24 And straightway the father of the child cried out, and said with tears, Lord, I believe; help thou mine unbelief.

Psalm 34:18
Amplified Bible

18
The Lord is near to the heartbroken
And He saves those who are crushed in spirit (contrite in heart, truly sorry for their sin).

Psalm 147:3
Amplified Bible[7]

3
He heals the brokenhearted
And binds up their wounds [healing their pain and comforting their sorrow].

Revelation 21:4
King James Version[8]

4 And God shall wipe away all tears from their eyes; and there shall be no more death, neither sorrow, nor crying, neither shall there be any more pain: for the former things are passed away.

2 Corinthians 1:3-8
American Standard Version[9]

3 Blessed be the God and Father of our Lord Jesus Christ, the Father of mercies and God of all comfort; 4 who comforteth us in all our affliction, that we may be able to comfort them that are in any affliction, through the comfort wherewith we ourselves are comforted of God. 5 For as the sufferings of Christ abound unto us, even so our comfort also aboundeth through Christ. 6 But whether we are afflicted, it is for your comfort and salvation; or whether we are comforted, it is for your comfort, which worketh in the patient enduring of the same sufferings which we also suffer: 7 and our hope for you is stedfast; knowing that, as ye are partakers of the sufferings, so also are ye of the comfort. 8 For we would not have you ignorant, brethren, concerning our affliction which befell us in Asia, that we were weighed down exceedingly, beyond our power, insomuch that we despaired even of life:

---

[8] King James Version (Public Domain)
[9] American Standard Version (Public Domain)

Rebuke Fear and Anxiety

Psalm 23
King James Version

23 The Lord is my shepherd; I shall not want.

2 He maketh me to lie down in green pastures: he leadeth me beside the still waters.

3 He restoreth my soul: he leadeth me in the paths of righteousness for his name's sake.

4 Yea, though I walk through the valley of the shadow of death, I will fear no evil: for thou art with me; thy rod and thy staff they comfort me.

5 Thou preparest a table before me in the presence of mine enemies: thou anointest my head with oil; my cup runneth over.

6 Surely goodness and mercy shall follow me all the days of my life: and I will dwell in the house of the Lord for ever.

Job 19:25-26
American Standard Version

25 But as for me I know that my Redeemer liveth,
And at last he will stand up upon the earth:
26 And after my skin, even this body, is destroyed,
Then without my flesh shall I see God;

Philippians 4:5-7
American Standard Version

5 Let your forbearance be known unto all men. The Lord is at hand. 6 In nothing be anxious; but in everything by prayer and supplication with thanksgiving let your requests be made known unto God. 7 And the peace of God, which passeth all understanding, shall guard your hearts and your thoughts in Christ Jesus.

1 Peter 5:7
American Standard Version[10]

7 casting all your anxiety upon him, because he careth for you.

Deuteronomy 31:6
King James Version

6 Be strong and of a good courage, fear not, nor be afraid of them: for the Lord thy God, he it is that doth go with thee; he will not fail thee, nor forsake thee.

---

[10] American Standard Version (Public Domain, BibleGateway.com)

Rebuke Cancer and Plagues

Psalm 91
American Standard Version

91 He that dwelleth in the secret place of the Most High
Shall abide under the shadow of the Almighty.
2 I will say of Jehovah, He is my refuge and my fortress;
My God, in whom I trust.
3 For he will deliver thee from the snare of the fowler,
And from the deadly pestilence.
4 He will cover thee with his pinions,
And under his wings shalt thou take refuge:
His truth is a shield and a buckler.
5 Thou shalt not be afraid for the terror by night,
Nor for the arrow that flieth by day;
6 For the pestilence that walketh in darkness,
Nor for the destruction that wasteth at noonday.
7 A thousand shall fall at thy side,
And ten thousand at thy right hand;
But it shall not come nigh thee.
8 Only with thine eyes shalt thou behold,
And see the reward of the wicked.
9 For thou, O Jehovah, art my refuge!
Thou hast made the Most High thy habitation;
10 There shall no evil befall thee,

Neither shall any plague come nigh thy tent.
11 For he will give his angels charge over thee,
To keep thee in all thy ways.
12 They shall bear thee up in their hands,
Lest thou dash thy foot against a stone.
13 Thou shalt tread upon the lion and adder:
The young lion and the serpent shalt thou trample under foot.
14 Because he hath set his love upon me, therefore will I deliver
him:
I will set him on high, because he hath known my name.
15 He shall call upon me, and I will answer him;
I will be with him in trouble:
I will deliver him, and honor him.
16 With long life will I satisfy him,
And show him my salvation.

Isaiah 40:31
American Standard Version

31 but they that wait for Jehovah shall renew their strength; they shall mount up with wings as eagles; they shall run, and not be weary; they shall walk, and not faint.

Matthew 11:28-29
King James Version

28 Come unto me, all ye that labour and are heavy laden, and I will give you rest. 29 Take my yoke upon you, and learn of me; for I am meek and lowly in heart: and ye shall find rest unto your souls.

According to Easton's Bible Dictionary, a plague is a stroke, or affliction, or disease.[11] The dictionary further defines a pestilential disease as an acute, malignant, and contagious disease. We see scriptural evidence regarding plagues in Exodus, Leviticus, Numbers, Deuteronomy, Mark, Luke, 1 Kings, and the psalms.

So, every plague is under the Blood of Jesus, under the protections listed in Psalm 91, and must Go!

---

[11] https://kingjamesbibledictionary.com/Dictionary/plague

Prayer Against Plagues

Abba Father, I praise You. I worship You. The God of Abraham, Isaac, and Jacob. The God of our precious Lord Jesus who died on the Cross for a sinner like me. I know by the blood Jesus shed on Calvary, that I have been set free of every disease, sickness, and plague. According to Psalm 91:3, You will deliver me from the snare of the fowler, and from the deadly pestilence. I believe in Your Word and declare Psalm 91:3 over my life. The devil must flee at the mention of Your Name. So, I say to you, satan, The Lord Jesus Rebukes you. Leave me now, leave my family, and never return. By the blood of Jesus, I am protected. My family is protected, and you have no right to come against me. So, with this prayer, I am declaring victory over every plague in my life based on Your work on the Cross. I love You, Jesus and know with this prayer, I am healed! In the powerful Name of Lord Jesus Christ, it is finished! Amen.

Refuse to Partner with Doubt and Unbelief

Doubt has no place in a believer's life. As Christians, we walk by faith and not by sight. We have power, love, and a sound mind.[12] When the devil tries to get us to doubt what God says about us, we only need to fight him with scripture as Jesus did in the wilderness (desert) when being tested by God right before He started His public ministry.[13]

The devil came at Jesus to tempt him while he was weak from fasting while being in the wilderness for forty days. Jesus had a physical need (hunger) and satan tried to exploit that need and use it against Jesus so God's plan of redemption through Jesus could be derailed. The devil (satan) tried to get Jesus to sin, like he did Adam and Eve in the garden, and he failed. Jesus Christ answered satan's questions with the Word of God. Jesus used His sword as we learned about in Ephesians 6 to defeat the enemy's deceptive lies.[14]

The devil tried to get Jesus to doubt God and act out of His emotions (feelings) at a moment of weakness, and probable frustration, and not God's perfect will. Basically, to disobey God's Word and commands. Jesus resisted the devil with the Truth, the Word of God, and he fled from Him. We must do the same! Let's look at Jesus as our guide the next time the devil comes at us at a moment of weakness and learn from scripture how to respond.

---

[12] 2 Timothy 1:7 (KJV, NIV)
[13] Mark 1: 12-15, Luke 4: 1-15
[14] Ephesians 6: 10-20

Matthew 4:1-11
King James Version

4 Then was Jesus led up of the Spirit into the wilderness to be tempted of the devil.

² And when he had fasted forty days and forty nights, he was afterward an hungred.

³ And when the tempter came to him, he said, If thou be the Son of God, command that these stones be made bread.

⁴ But he answered and said, It is written, Man shall not live by bread alone, but by every word that proceedeth out of the mouth of God.

⁵ Then the devil taketh him up into the holy city, and setteth him on a pinnacle of the temple,

⁶ And saith unto him, If thou be the Son of God, cast thyself down: for it is written, He shall give his angels charge concerning thee: and in their hands they shall bear thee up, lest at any time thou dash thy foot against a stone.

⁷ Jesus said unto him, It is written again, Thou shalt not tempt the Lord thy God.

⁸ Again, the devil taketh him up into an exceeding high mountain, and sheweth him all the kingdoms of the world, and the glory of them;

⁹ And saith unto him, All these things will I give thee, if thou wilt fall down and worship me.

¹⁰ Then saith Jesus unto him, Get thee hence, Satan: for it is written, Thou shalt worship the Lord thy God, and him only shalt thou serve.

¹¹ Then the devil leaveth him, and, behold, angels came and ministered unto him.

Ephesians 6: 10-20
King James Version

¹⁰ Finally, my brethren, be strong in the Lord, and in the power of his might.

¹¹ Put on the whole armour of God, that ye may be able to stand against the wiles of the devil.

¹² For we wrestle not against flesh and blood, but against principalities, against powers, against the rulers of the darkness of this world, against spiritual wickedness in high places.

¹³ Wherefore take unto you the whole armour of God, that ye may be able to withstand in the evil day, and having done all, to stand.

¹⁴ Stand therefore, having your loins girt about with truth, and having on the breastplate of righteousness;

¹⁵ And your feet shod with the preparation of the gospel of peace;

¹⁶ Above all, taking the shield of faith, wherewith ye shall be able to quench all the fiery darts of the wicked.

¹⁷ And take the helmet of salvation, and the sword of the Spirit, which is the word of God:

¹⁸ Praying always with all prayer and supplication in the Spirit, and watching thereunto with all perseverance and supplication for all saints;

¹⁹ And for me, that utterance may be given unto me, that I may open my mouth boldly, to make known the mystery of the gospel,

²⁰ For which I am an ambassador in bonds: that therein I may speak boldly, as I ought to speak.

James 4:7
King James Version
Submit yourselves therefore to God. Resist the devil, and he will flee from you.

Mark 5:36
New Living Translation
But Jesus overheard them and said to Jairus, "Don't be afraid. Just have faith."

Mark 11:22-26
King James Version

22 And Jesus answering saith unto them, Have faith in God.

23 For verily I say unto you, That whosoever shall say unto this mountain, Be thou removed, and be thou cast into the sea; and shall not doubt in his heart, but shall believe that those things which he saith shall come to pass; he shall have whatsoever he saith.

24 Therefore I say unto you, What things soever ye desire, when ye pray, believe that ye receive them, and ye shall have them.

25 And when ye stand praying, forgive, if ye have ought against any: that your Father also which is in heaven may forgive you your trespasses.

26 But if ye do not forgive, neither will your Father which is in heaven forgive your trespasses.

Holy Communion

Communion is such a sacred act of worship and brings healing. When we partake of communion, whether as a group or a solo act in our home, we are recognizing that Lord Jesus Christ died on the Cross so we could be made whole (healed). Christ's body was broken, battered, bruised, pierced for our inequities, our sin. By His thirty-nine stripes, we were healed. Now, let's let scripture guide us with this practice.

Matthew 26:26–29 (ESV)
Institution of the Lord's Supper

[26] Now as they were eating, Jesus took bread, and after blessing it broke it and gave it to the disciples, and said, "Take, eat; this is my body." [27] And he took a cup, and when he had given thanks he gave it to them, saying, "Drink of it, all of you, [28] for this is my blood of the covenant, which is poured out for many for the forgiveness of sins. [29] I tell you I will not drink again of this fruit of the vine until that day when I drink it new with you in my Father's kingdom."

1 Corinthians 11:23–26 (ESV)

[23] For I received from the Lord what I also delivered to you, that the Lord Jesus on the night when he was betrayed took bread, [24] and when he had given thanks, he broke it, and said, "This is my body, which is for you. Do this in remembrance of me." [25] In the same way also he took the cup, after supper, saying, "This cup is the new covenant in my blood. Do this, as often as you drink it, in remembrance of me." [26] For as often as you eat this bread and drink the cup, you proclaim the Lord's death until he comes.

1 Corinthians 11:28 (ESV)

28 Let a person examine himself, then, and so eat of the bread and drink of the cup.

Communion gives us a time to look inward and reflect before the Lord. We can examine ourselves (actions, words, motives) and see if they are an example of how Christ lived and died (unselfish, pure in heart, humble, compassionate, merciful, agape love).

"Whoever partakes of the Lord's Supper must examine himself to see whether he has properly understood the unselfish, atoning nature of Jesus's death "for" others, and how that should be
imitated in his own life."[15]

After examining ourselves, we can humble ourselves before the Lord and ask Him to cleanse us of all unrighteousness (Read Psalm 19), purge us of any hidden or secret sin, and confess that we may have "missed it." Ask Lord Jesus to help us have His heart and mind and to walk in a posture of obedience to His will and not ours. We can repent, if we need to, and turn away from sin (rebellion, disobedience), trust His work on the Cross, and walk in His way of Truth.

Communion recognizes that Jesus is the Bread of Life and is our Sustainer and Redeemer. Through His Body (Bread) being broken and His Blood shed on Calvary (cup), we are under the New Covenant of grace, and reconciled with God, through His Son, Lord Jesus Christ. By partaking in this act, we recognize His

---

[15] Crossway.org, May 2024

Sovereignty (Yeshua, over our lives and offer praise to Him and God the Father (Adonai) for sending His Son to die on the Cross in our place.

Isaiah 53:5 (NLT)

5 But he was pierced for our rebellion,
crushed for our sins.
He was beaten so we could be whole.
He was whipped so we could be healed.

Communion is a time of praise and worship, not an obligation, but a celebration. Communion celebrates the Gospel: Jesus was broken for us so that we can be fixed by Him. Celebrating communion marks the story of Jesus, in which He gave Himself completely to give us a better life, a new start, and a fresh relationship with God (1 Peter 3:18). It's not about a ritual to revere, but a person to worship. Jesus is less concerned about the method of celebrating communion and more concerned that we celebrate it. As often as we remember Jesus, we should celebrate Jesus.[16] Do you need Communion elements like are provided for you at church? No, you can get a little juice and break a piece of bread, and that will be fine. The important part is that you are doing it as an act of worship and praise for the Lamb's sacrifice so we can have an abundant life! You are saying, "Jesus, I love you and am so grateful you died for me. "Father, I am so grateful that you sent Jesus to die for me."

Sinner's Prayer to be Saved

---

[16] Living Word.net

Dear Heavenly Father,

I come to you in the Name of Jesus. Your Word says, "The one who comes to Me I will by no means cast out" (John 6:37 NKJV). I know You won't cast me out or turn me away. I know You take me in and I am grateful for You and thank You. You said in Your Word, "Whoever calls on the name of the Lord shall be saved" (Romans 10:13 NKJV). I am calling on Your Name, now, Oh Lord, and I believe You have saved me, a lost sinner. You also state in Your Word, in Romans 10: 9-10, "If you confess with your mouth the Lord Jesus and believe in your heart that God has raised Him from the dead, you will be saved. For with the heart, one believes unto righteousness, and with the mouth of confession is made unto salvation." I believe Jesus rose from the dead for my justification. I am now reconciled to God. I confess Jesus as My Lord and Savior. Because Your Word says that "with the heart one believes unto righteousness," and I do believe with my heart, I have now become the righteousness of God in Christ (2 Corinthians 5:21). I now know I have been redeemed, restored, saved by the blood of Jesus.

Thank You, Lord Jesus. I praise and honor You and believe with this prayer and declaration that the Holy Spirit, Your Spirit, lives inside of me, making me fresh, clean, and new. I surrender to God's will for my life, instead of my will. Thank You, God, for giving me the heart and mind of Christ, for washing me clean, and setting me free.

If you prayed this prayer, welcome to the family! Please email us at info@reflectivespacesministry.com to discuss next steps and mail you out resources for your walk as a new Christian.

(Prayer adapted from Kenneth E. Hagin's Laying on of Hands Book, pg. 33, Rhema Bible Church).

About the Author

Reflective Spaces Ministry, Corp, is a 501(c)(3) non-profit founded in 2021 by Tammy Toney-Butler, a former emergency department nurse and sexual assault nurse examiner. Following the whisper of the Holy Spirit, she and her husband relocated to Lee County, Florida. They purchased a ten-acre parcel of land to begin a trauma-focused, healing ministry.

Tammy, a Healing Evangelist, can be found on the streets, going after the ones. Tammy's lived experience provides a unique teaching style and trauma-focused lens perspective, offering survivors environments conducive to healing mind, body, and spirit.

Tammy Toney-Butler, as a teenager, survived the loss of her father to suicide. She overcame being a victim of child sex trafficking and coping with the aftermath of trauma through various addictions through her faith in the Lord Jesus and is a powerful testimony of faith in action.

In 2023, Reflective Hour with Tammy Toney-Butler was launched in podcast and YouTube formats as a platform for transformational healing in Christ. The Reflective Spaces Ministry podcast was launched in podcast and YouTube formats in 2024.

Tammy is outspoken in her mission to provide a trauma-responsive pulpit and a compassionate, merciful lens through which one offers pastoral support. Love is her focus because the love of Jesus Christ heals all wounds, delivers, and transforms.

Tammy has become the mouthpiece for God's message of hope and healing worldwide. She is a published author whose works have been featured in the National Library of Medicine, Congress.gov, textbooks, and several professional journals.

Her memoir and healing devotional with journal pages are available on Amazon and Kindle.

Tammy has spoken at the United Nations, American Nurses Association (ANA) General Assembly, ANA New York, ANA Georgia, ANA Vermont, and has been a guest on network television.

From the ranch to the pulpit, from the trailer park to the assembly hall, God has moved mightily in Tammy's life, and the Lord Jesus Christ gets all the credit and honor for her transformation and restoration.

Contact Information

Tammy Toney-Butler,
Reflective Spaces Ministry, Corp, 16295 S. Tamiami Trail, Suite
133, Fort Myers, FL 33908
info@reflectivespacesministry.com
www.reflectivespacesministry.com

www.reflectivespacespodcast.com

Reflective Hour with Tammy Toney-Butler is available at:
www.reflectivehour.com

You can purchase her book on Amazon Kindle, "When you
know, that you know, that you know there is a God."
https://www.amazon.com/stores/Tammy-Toney-
Butler/author/B0DC1VXP45?ref=ap_rdr&isDramIntegrated=t
rue&shoppingPortalEnabled=true

About Tammy:
https://www.reflectivespacesministry.com/about

Tammy is available to teach and empower women and men as
they journey to wholeness through the Light and Love of Christ.
Contact her to book an in-person prophetic healing session,
meeting, service, or conference at www.tammytoneybutler.com

Hotline Support

Hotline numbers:
https://www.reflectivespacesministry.com/contact

National Human Trafficking Hotline
1-888-373-7888

Report Human Trafficking in Florida, call 1-855-352-7233
1 (855) FLA-SAFE

Report Human Trafficking in Georgia, call 1-866-363-4842

National Center on Missing and Exploited Children Cyber Tip
Line
1-800-THE-LOST
1-800-843-5678

Suicide & Crisis Lifeline
988

National Sexual Assault Hotline
1-800-656-4673

National Teen Dating Abuse Hotline
1-866-331-9474

Runaway Hotline
1-800-786-2929

Domestic Violence Hotline
1-800-799-7233

Department of Homeland Security to Report Human Trafficking
1-866-347-2423

Need Training on Human Trafficking, Trauma, and Exploitation
Contact
Nurses United Against Human Trafficking, PA
www.nuaht.org
info@nuaht.org

Reflective Spaces Ministry, Corp

Reflective Spaces Ministry, Corp, is a 501(c)(3) non-profit founded in 2021 by Tammy Toney-Butler, a former emergency department nurse and sexual assault nurse examiner. Following the Holy Spirit's whisper, she and her husband, David, relocated to Lee County, Florida. They purchased a ten-acre parcel of land to begin a trauma-focused, healing ministry.

The mission of Reflective Spaces Ministry is to provide reflective spaces for transformational healing and total restoration in a faith-filled environment for survivors of human trafficking, sexual violence, domestic violence, and childhood adversity to thrive. In 2025, our Founder, Tammy Toney-Butler, on her journey to wholeness, had an awakening as to the fundamental mission of Reflective Spaces Ministry.

Our goal is to show the heart of Christ to all we encounter, empowering and enabling them with the strength and courage required to look inward, reflect on the past adversities faced, and live transformed lives despite it. A reflective space within one's own heart, full of strength, power, and courage to face the dark, refuse to let it break them, and instead, process and overcome it one layer at a time. Bringing them to wholeness, physically, mentally, spiritually, and financially.

Consider donating to our direct survivor assistance programs, including day programs such as respite retreats for spiritual renewal through nature, as well as free healing ministry services. The team believes in empowering every survivor with a safe retreat experience in a private setting while they process the dark and transition into the Light. Survivor empowerment is vital to recovery; assisting survivors/thrivers with transportation and living expenses as they transition on their healing journey is vital to long-term success.

Reflective Spaces Ministry assesses and meets them where they are on their healing journey, whatever that looks like for their unique situation. Finding gaps in existing services and bridging those ensures an overall positive transitional health experience. Overcoming barriers to care and supplying Maslow's Basic Hierarchy of Needs ensures that youth transitioning into adulthood and vulnerable adults will not be left behind. "Throw-Away" youth are vulnerable to trafficking and exploitation; thus, wrap-around support is needed to bridge gaps and provide pathways for success.

Positive mentoring, role modeling, and empowerment are essential for this generation of young warriors to tap into their hidden purpose and become all God has called them to be in this stage of their lives. Positive childhood experiences (PACES), such as a day retreat at A&K Ranch, can help mitigate the effects of adverse childhood experiences (ACES). Empowering "thrivers" with resources and choices as they journey to wholeness is a mission worthy of your financial support.

Sow A Seed: Donate

Consider SOWING A SEED to further our community outreach and evangelism efforts to spread the Gospel worldwide! Even if the ninety-nine are safe, we go after the one! Partner with our ministry by clicking on the ministry link below to help us gather the ones into the family of Light.

https://www.reflectivespacesministry.com/

https://www.paypal.com/fundraiser/charity/4406377

https://account.venmo.com/u/Reflectivespacesministry

Nurses United Against Human Trafficking, PA

Nurses United Against Human Trafficking (NUAHT) was founded in 2020 by two nurses driven to abolish modern-day slavery. Dr. Francine Bono-Neri and Tammy Toney-Butler. NUAHT offers education modules, membership resources, and consulting services for healthcare professionals, by building human trafficking protocols and community response teams. [17]

The mission of NUAHT is to eradicate human trafficking by raising awareness, providing education and resources, and participating in advocacy efforts, all for the hope of emboldening and empowering healthcare professionals, by establishing best practices and standards of care for this vulnerable and invisible population.[18]

For every membership purchased, NUAHT donates to Reflective Spaces Ministry, a direct service provider for survivors of human trafficking, sexual and physical violence, and childhood adversity (trauma). Reflective Spaces Ministry provides all services for free.

---

[17] www.nuaht.org

[18] https://www.nursesunitedagainsthumantrafficking.org/

Note from the Author

As a survivor of child sex trafficking and loss of father to suicide as a teenager, I know trauma and loss all too well. Our ministry, Reflective Spaces Ministry, focuses on hope and healing, one layer at a time. Through quiet reflection and inner work, one can achieve wholeness through faith in the Lord Jesus Christ, as I have done by His grace and mercy on my life. As a Healing Evangelist, my heart is for the lost, broken, wounded, and those coping with trauma through various addictions. Love heals and transforms, as evidenced by our Lord and Savior, Jesus Christ. My goal, His goal, is to empower, inform, and equip with the tools needed to thrive as maturity through faith increases, and deliverance is possible.

I am not just interested in getting them out of Egypt but getting Egypt out of them. A renewed mind is possible, with ultimate healing in four key areas of fitness: spiritual, mental, physical, and financial. Achieving wholeness is possible if one puts the work in. Trauma destroyed my family, and I am on a mission to save yours and all those I encounter. Breaking generational patterns of abuse is an essential component of healing, trauma work, and a focus of our ministry.

Thank you again for trusting me to deliver a healing message to you by way of His books.

Blessings and Peace,

Tammy Toney-Butler, Healing Evangelist

Bible Versions and Abbreviations

English Standard Version (ESV), Crossway, A Publishing ministry of Good News Ministry.

King James Version (KJV), Public Domain.

Amplified Bible (AMP), The Lockman Foundation. 2015.

Complete Jewish Bible (CJB), David H. Stern, 1998.

Easy-to-Read Version (ERV), Bible League International, 2006.

The Message Bible (MSG), 1993, 2002, 2018, Eugene H. Peterson

New Living Translation (NLT), Tyndale House Publishers, 1996, 2004, 2015

Tree of Life Version (TLV), Messianic Jewish Family Bible Society, 2015.

New International Version (NIV), Biblica, Inc., 1973, 1978, 1984, 2011.

Also used as references BibleGateway.com.

What are you grateful for today? Remember to journal and give thanks today for what God has already done in your life. Remember what He brought you out of and pat yourself on the back. You have come so far, and you should be proud of yourself.

Accomplishments

What did you accomplish today? Did you get out of bed, brush your teeth? Make your bed? Wash the dishes? These are big things to someone who struggles with depression. Celebrate your baby steps and keep on stepping. Journal your accomplishments. Look at the positive instead of the negative. Get rid of old mindsets and pray to have the mind of Christ.

www.ingramcontent.com/pod-product-compliance
Lightning Source LLC
Chambersburg PA
CBHW081643040426

42449CB00015B/3437

9798994590706